Rock Your Party

Laura Torres

QED

QED Publishing

Editor: Eve Marleau
Designer: Lisa Peacock
Photographer: Simon Pask
Project Maker: Dani Hall

Printed in China

Contents

Get the basics

Sometimes, the best thing about a party is the preparation. Why not add some personal pizzazz to your party? With a few materials, you can turn your party into a one-of-a-kind event.

Many of the projects use items that you have around the house. But if you don't have exactly what you need, improvise! For example, you could use scraps of paper instead of tissue paper for the Birthday Wreath. Some projects also work as fun party activities.

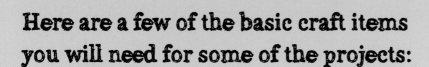

Here are a few of the basic craft items
you will need for some of the projects:

Scissors - Make sure you always have a good pair of scissors for cutting things such as paper, felt and wool in the projects.

Card - Card is cheap and comes in all kinds of colours, but you can use any coloured paper as a substitute.

Curling ribbon - This is ribbon that has ridges on it. When you run it over the blade of a pair of scissors, it curls. Always ask an adult for help when you curl ribbon.

Glue - If a project calls for 'glue' you can use whatever you might have around the house. 'White glue' means a white standard glue. 'Craft glue' means a thick white glue that won't run or spread.

Always remember...
When crafting, be sure you protect the surface you are working on with newspaper or plastic for easy clean-up.

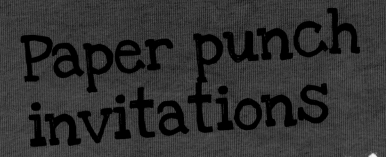

Paper punch invitations

YOU WILL NEED

- Hole punch
- Four different colours of paper
- Card
- Scissors
- Glue
- Thin marker
- Ruler

Get your party started the right way with some unique party invitations.

↑ If you are having a fancy dress theme, such as pirates, why not turn the balloon into a skull and crossbones?

Step 1

Cut the card into 6 x 12 centimetre pieces. Fold each piece in half.

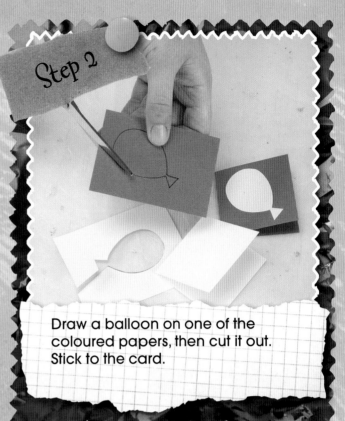

Step 2

Draw a balloon on one of the coloured papers, then cut it out. Stick to the card.

Step 3

Punch holes in the coloured papers, then stick these circles to the balloon shape.

Step 4

Draw strings on the balloons and write the party details inside the card.

Birthday wreath

YOU WILL NEED
- Three colours of crêpe paper
- Scissors
- Wire coat hanger

Hang this wreath on your front door to welcome guests to your party.

Turn your fluffy wreath into a monster by drawing a funny face on a piece of card and taping it into the middle.

Step 1

Bend the coat hanger into a circle. It doesn't have to be perfect. Ask an adult to help you bend it with some pliers if it's too stiff.

Step 2

Cut pieces of the different-coloured crêpe papers into strips.

Step 3

Twist each strip once in the middle, so it looks like a bow tie.

Step 4

Centre each strip underneath the coat hanger wire and twist it once around the wire. Keep doing this until the wreath is full and fluffy.

Fingerprint thank-yous

These mini masterpieces make great personalized thank-you cards. They could also be used as party invites.

Try drawing bow ties to give your thank-yous a formal look.

Step 1

Cut out the cards into 6 x 12 centimetre pieces. Fold the long edge in half to make the card.

Step 2

Pour a small amount of the poster paint into the plastic dish. Press your finger into the paint. Now press it onto the front of the card.

Step 3

When the paint is dry, draw funny faces on the fingerprints.

Step 4

Cut party hats out of the coloured paper and glue them on your fingerprint heads.

Step 5

Use the felt-tip pens to draw hair on your fingerprint heads, then write your message inside.

Sock friend

YOU WILL NEED

- One sock for each guest
- Scissors
- Uncooked rice
- Rubber bands
- Black and white felt
- Pom poms
- Red or pink wool
- Craft glue

Have each party guest bring an old sock, or provide a sock for each person for this fun make and take-home gift.

Try swapping sock 'hats' between sock friends to mix it up.

Step 1

Cut the sock in two, just below the heel.

Step 2

Fill the sock about two-thirds full of rice. Close the open end of the sock by wrapping it tightly with a rubber band.

Step 3

Cut the heel off the other part of the sock. Turn the rest of the sock inside out and tie the cut end with a rubber band.

Step 4

Turn the sock right-side out to make a hat. Put the hat on the 'head' of the sock.

Step 5

Cut eyes out of the felt and glue in place. Glue on a pom pom nose and a wool mouth. Let dry.

13

Newspaper party hats

Ask a friend or an adult to help you make these cool hats in preparation for your party.

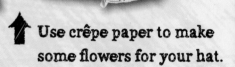

Use crêpe paper to make some flowers for your hat.

Step 1

For each hat, unfold five or six pieces of newspaper. Stack them with each sheet at a different angle, so they are fanned out.

Step 2

Put the paper on your friend's head. Press the paper down all around the top of their head to form the top of the hat.

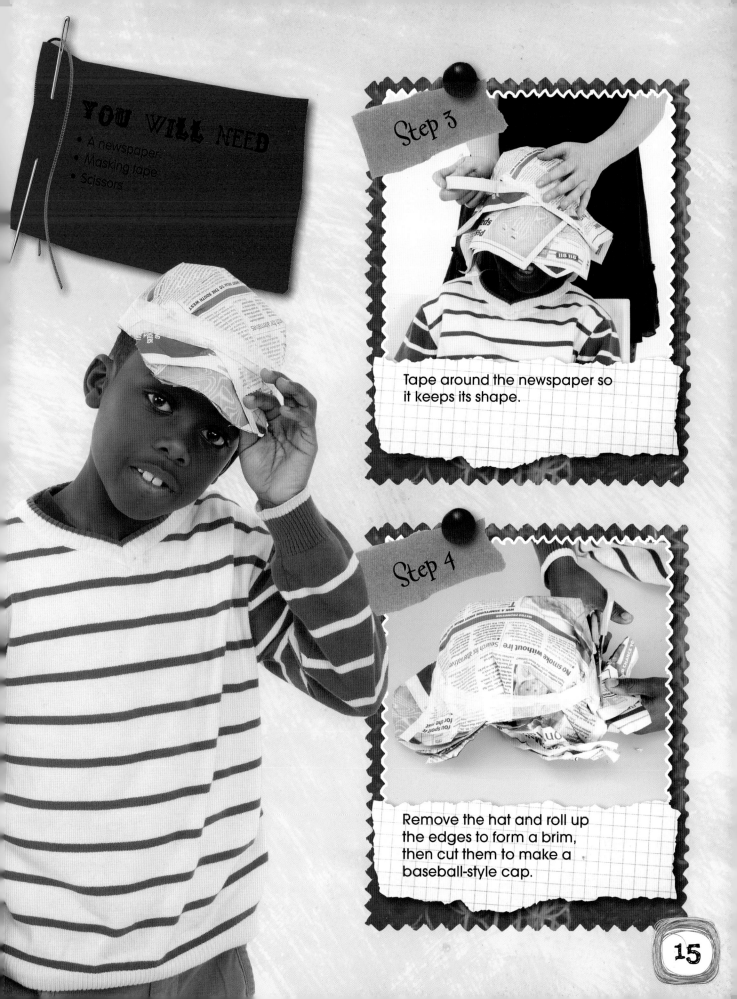

YOU WILL NEED

- A newspaper
- Masking tape
- Scissors

Step 3

Tape around the newspaper so it keeps its shape.

Step 4

Remove the hat and roll up the edges to form a brim, then cut them to make a baseball-style cap.

Balloon favour bags

Fill favour bags ahead of the party with sweet treats or small toys so your guests can take them home as a souvenir.

Eddie

Claire

Step 1

Ed

Write each guest's name at the bottom of a bag with the marker.

16

Try cutting different-shaped ears to make different kinds of animal.

Step 2

Put some sweets or small toys inside each paper sack. Fold the top one-third of the way down and staple shut.

Step 3

Cut out a nose, ears and eyes for each sack out of coloured card.

Step 4

Eddie

Glue the features in place on the folded-down part of the bag. You can make them all the same, or make each one different.

Step 5

Eddie

Cut whiskers from the wool then stick next to the nose. Let dry.

Monster Piñata

A piñata is a fun party favourite. Why not give it a twist by turning it into a scary monster?

➡ Use bright green for a scary-looking monster!

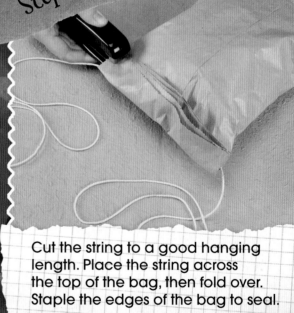

Step 1

Fill one paper bag about half full of sweets and toys. Ball up some newspapers and stuff the sack until it is three-quarters full.

Step 2

Cut the string to a good hanging length. Place the string across the top of the bag, then fold over. Staple the edges of the bag to seal.

Step 3

Make a paste by adding some water to the flour in the bowl, then dip the newspaper into it. Cover the bag with the strips, then paint with paste.

Step 4

When the newspaper is totally dry (this might take a few hours), paint the piñata a bright colour. Let dry.

Step 5

Cut some paper to make arms and legs, and then some more skinny strips of paper for hair. Tape in place, then paint a silly face.

Wool party pals

These fun friends double as a party activity and a take-home gift. Everyone will find these quick and easy to make.

Cut a piece of cardboard about 12 x 6 centimetres.

Wrap wool around the width of the cardboard until you have a thick bundle. You can change colours or make it all the same.

Step 3

Cut the end of the wool. Carefully remove the bundle from the cardboard.

Step 4

Cut a piece of wool about 12 centimetres long. Tie it tightly around the middle of the wool bundle.

Step 5

Cut through the loops of wool on each side. Fluff and trim any stray ends. Cut out eyes from the felt and glue on to the wool to make a face.

Try using your school or sports team's colours.

21

Balloon ball toss

Make these simple balloon balls and game before the party. Have some small prizes on hand for the winners.

Step 1

Insert the funnel into a balloon. Gradually pour sugar into the funnel so it goes into the balloon. Tie a knot in the end.

Step 2

Cut the ends off three other balloons. Stretch one balloon over the filled balloon, starting at the knotted end. Repeat with the other two balloons.

Step 3

Write a point value for each box on a piece of coloured paper. Tape the papers to the front of the boxes.

Step 4

To play, each player takes turns tossing the three balls into the boxes. The player with the highest score wins.

You can decorate the boxes with wrapping paper.

Tissue-paper party puffs

Hang these colourful party decorations from the ceiling or from tree branches if your party is outside.

➡ Use different-coloured tissue paper to make puffs the same colours as your favourite sports team.

Step 1

Cut the tissue paper to about 50 x 50 centimetres. You will need ten pieces per puff.

Step 2

Place ten pieces of tissue paper in a neat stack. Starting with one edge, fold the stack a few times with the folds about 4–5 centimetres wide.

Step 3

Wrap a twist-tie around the middle of the tissue. Thread the wool under the wire and make in a knot. Cut to the right length for hanging the puff.

Step 4

Use the pinking shears or the scissors to trim the edges of the tissue.

Step 5

Separate the layers of tissue very carefully into a puff. Make several more puffs and hang up.

Curly name tags

Curly
name tags

YOU WILL NEED
- Dark blue or purple paper or card
- Scissors
- Metallic markers
- Double-sided tape
- Curling ribbon
- Hole punch
- Glue
- Flat-backed rhinestones

Make these party-perfect name tags for all your guests – it's a great way to introduce yourself and make new friends.

If you're having a Christmas party, why not try using red, white and green for a festive look?

Ben

Sarah

Step 1

For each name tag, cut the paper or card to 6 x16 centimetres. Fold the nametag in half, long edge down.

Step 2

Cut pieces of curling ribbon in different colours and lengths. Ask an adult to help you curl the ribbon with the scissors.

Step 3

Tape the ends of the ribbon inside with the curls sticking out the sides. Put a piece of tape in the middle and stick the sides together.

Step 4

Punch a hole on each side of the name tag and thread a long piece of ribbon through the holes. Tie the ends to make a necklace.

Step 5

Glue some flat-backed rhinestones to the front, then write your guests names in the centre.

Happy birthday garland

String these garlands inside a door or window frame, or hang them over the party table.

Step 1

Trace around the bowl or large mug on card to make a circle pattern for the letters. Cut out the pattern.

Step 2

Trace around the pattern and cut out enough circles to spell out your name, or 'Happy Birthday'. Write the letters on each circle.

Use bright pinks and purples for a girly sleep over.

YOU WILL NEED

- Coloured card
- Bowl or large mug
- Pencil
- Fishing line or string
- Tape
- Markers
- Scissors
- Hole punch

Step 3

Punch two holes in the top of each circle, about 2 centimetres apart.

Step 4

String each letter onto the fishing line or string. Put a piece of tape over the string on the back of each circle to hold them in place.

Step 5

Using the tape, hang your garland by a window or on a wall.

If you don't have everything you need for the projects in this book, there's no need to worry – you can customize each item with what you have around the house.

Party punch invitations

Use recycled paper to make your punches. Junk mail and magazine pages are often colourful, and you only need a tiny bit of each colour.

Newspaper party hats

If you don't have any newspaper to recycle, you can try used wrapping paper, packing paper, tissue paper, or whatever you might have around the house.

Sock friend

There is no need to buy new socks for this project if you collect odd socks, or socks that are too small.

Pages 20 and 26

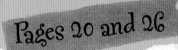

Birthday wreath and tissue-party puffs

Save tissue paper and crêpe paper decorations from parties to recycle into these new decorations. There's no need to throw the decorations away after the party when you can reuse them!

Page 28

Birthday garland

Instead of using new card to make the circles, you can cut them from items such as cereal boxes.

Recycled wrapping

Get creative with wrapping a present for a party using material you already have around the house. Try bubble wrap, the comic pages of the newspaper, or a plain bag that you have decorated with stickers.

Index

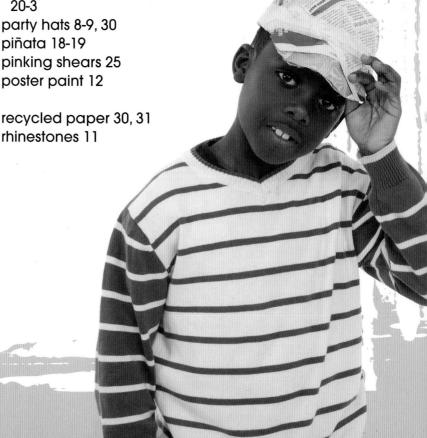